You Are
LOVED

You Are LOVED

A Four-Week
Bible Study for Teens

Lisa Fahey

Farmhouse
Publishings

For information on distribution rights, royalties, derivative works, or licensing opportunities on behalf of this content or work, please get in touch with the publisher at the address below:

Farmhouse Publishings, LLC
P.O. Box 333
Spearfish, SD 57783

Scripture quotations taken from the (NASB®) New American Standard Bible®, Copyright © 1960, 1971, 1977, 1995, 2020 by The Lockman Foundation. Used by permission. All rights reserved. lockman.org. Scripture quotations taken from the Holy Bible, New International Version®, NIV® Copyright © 1973, 1978, 1984, 2011 by Biblica, Inc.Used with permission. All rights reserved worldwide.

Although the author and publisher have tried to ensure that the information and advice in this book were correct and accurate at press time, the author and publisher do not assume and disclaim any liability to any party for any loss, damage, or disruption caused by acting upon the information in this book or by errors or omissions, whether such errors or omissions result from negligence, accident, or any other cause.

ISBN # 979-8-9918470-8-7

Cover Art by Stephanie Allard
Layout and Design by Heidi Caperton

Printed in the United States of America.

To our beautiful daughters, Alisha and Rebecca,

You inspire me every single day to become
a better version of myself.

You are two of the most extraordinary women I have ever
known, and I am endlessly proud of who you are.

Thank you for the precious gift of allowing me to be your mother.

May you always carry this truth in your hearts: you are
beautiful, wonderfully made, and deeply loved.

With all my love,

Mom

Table of Contents

How This Works

This study was created just for you—to remind you that God deeply loves you and that your life has a purpose.

Each week, we'll walk through a short lesson focusing on a key truth about God's love and your identity in Him. There will be:

- A Bible passage to read.
- A short teaching to help you understand how it applies to your life.
- A prayer.
- A few reflection questions to help you think and go deeper
- A simple challenge at the end of each week to live out what you've learned.

- Scan the QR code to listen to the You Are Loved playlist on Spotify—it's filled with songs to remind you that you are loved. Enjoy the music as you go through the study!

You can go through this on your own, with a friend, or in a small group. There's no pressure to have all the answers—this is about learning, growing, and knowing that you are not alone.

Be honest. Ask questions. Write what's on your heart.

Introduction

I'm the oldest in my family and grew up with three younger siblings. Life was good—until one day, it suddenly wasn't. Our family experienced a life-changing event that completely flipped everything upside down. Maybe you've experienced that too—when life changes and nothing feels secure anymore. If you haven't experienced that, praise the Lord—and thank your parents. Seriously!

It is at times like these that we start asking ourselves hard questions: "Who am I really?" "Do I matter?" "Am I enough?"

I used to think my worth came from the people I could make happy and the titles I worked hard to achieve. Being good at what I did and how others saw me shaped my identity. I believed I was valuable as long as I kept performing well. But a shift in my career—a conflict with my boss at a church I was working at—tested that belief. I made the difficult decision to step down. Suddenly, I felt, like a failure. I imagined everyone was disappointed in me. I began questioning everything about myself.

That experience forced me to face a truth I hadn't really grasped before: My worth isn't found in titles, applause, or performance. It's found in who God says I am.

Working with teens for over thirty years has taught me that I'm not alone in grappling with this issue. So many of us—quiet or loud, confident or uncertain—wonder if we're really lovable, if we're enough, or if we matter.

This message is for you—if you've ever felt that way.

The world tells us we must earn attention, love, and approval. We are often told to be the best athlete, the smartest student, the funniest friend, or the hardest worker. But let me ask you this: if you lost all of those things, would you still be valuable?

Yes. Absolutely, yes.

Your existence is because you are a child of God. God created you with purpose and intention. Even when the world forgets to clap for you, God never stops calling you His. You don't have to prove yourself. You are already deeply known and completely loved.

Lisa

He will never leave you
nor forsake you.

—Deuteronomy 31:8 (NASB)

Week One

OVERLOOKED

Have you ever felt like life is racing by, yet you're stuck standing still, just watching it all happen? Kind of like everyone else is getting to join in on something fun, you're the one left behind?

That happened to me one totally normal day while I was cleaning the house (I know, not exactly a "deep moment" vibe). Out of nowhere, I felt this emptiness, like I was missing something important—but I didn't know what it was.

Then it hit me.

I had been so busy—caught up in my daily never-ending to-do lists. I had pushed God out to the edges of my life, not on purpose.

But still, He felt far away. What are you busy and caught up in _____ (fill in your season: School? Sports? Drama with friends? Or just everything?)

Read Isaiah 43:4. (If you don't have a Bible with you, no problem! Just grab your phone and go to BibleGateway.com. You can search for any Bible verse there. Look for the NASB or NIV versions—they're easy to read and understand).

God calls you **precious** and **honored**. And here's the best part:

"Because I love you."

Those four words? They're the heartbeat of the whole Bible—one big, beautiful love letter from God to *you*.

Sometimes, when we feel left out, we're afraid of something deeper—we wonder if *God* has overlooked us. But He hasn't. Not even for a second. You don't have to fight for His attention. You already *have* it.

Read Psalm 139:1–18

Take your time with this one. It's packed with truth:

- God sees you.
- God knows your thoughts.
- God designed every little part of you—on purpose.

You're not random. You're not forgotten. **You are *known*.**

Read Isaiah 49:16

What do you think? God has your name written on His hands—like it's tattooed there. That means you matter to Him. You're always close to His heart, and He'll never forget you.

And just in case you ever doubt it...

John 3:16 tells us the *proof* of God's love: He gave *everything*—His Son—for *you*. That's not the kind of love that forgets people. That's the kind of love that *rescues* people.

This week, whenever you feel overlooked or invisible, stop and remind yourself:

YOU MATTER TO GOD.

He sees you. He hears you. He loves you—right here, right now.

Want more? Check out:

- **Romans 5:8** – God loved you even before you loved Him.
- **Romans 8:35–39** – Nothing can separate you from God's love.
- **1 John 4:16** – God *is* love.

Prayer:

Heavenly Father,

Love can be really hard. I want to love You more, and I want to love others—but if I'm honest, sometimes it's even hard to love myself. Please show me what real love looks like. Help me become the person You created me to be, and give me the courage to share Your love with others. Be with me when it's tough to love—even those who love me. And when I feel alone or not enough, remind me that You are always with me and that Your love for me never changes. Amen.

Discussion Questions:

What happens to your time with God when life gets busy or overwhelming?

Be honest—do you ever doubt that God really, *truly* loves you? Why or why not?

How do you think God sees you? Is that different from how *you* see you?

Journaling Prompt – "Seen by God"

Find a quiet spot (yes, even five minutes counts) and write about this:

"God, do You really see me?" Write your honest thoughts—whatever comes to mind.

Then, reread **Psalm 139:1–18** and write down three truths that stood out to you.

Finish your entry by writing this sentence: *"I am not overlooked. I am seen, known, and loved by You."*

_____

_____

_____

_____

_____

_____

_____

_____

Overlooked

Faith in Focus: Doodle Your Thoughts

Journaling Prompt – "When I Feel Invisible"

Ever have one of those days where it feels like no one sees you? Like you're just in the background and no one really notices or cares? Yeah, those moments can hit hard—and they can start to shape the way we think about ourselves.

But here's something to hold onto: God sees you. Every time. And He *never* overlooks you.

Think back to a time when you felt left out or unseen—maybe at school, with friends, or even at home.

- What was happening in that moment?
- How did it make you feel?
- What thoughts did you have about yourself because of it?

Take a few minutes to write it all out. Be real. This is just between you and God.

Faith in Focus: Doodle Your Thoughts

Social Challenge - #YouAreLovedChallenge

This week, try this challenge on your favorite platform (or just in your group chat or stories):

Post a pic or a note with the caption:

"Even when I feel invisible, God sees me. #YouAreLovedChallenge #NotOverlooked"

Want to go next level? Tag a friend and encourage them with something *you* see that's special or God-given in them. Something like:

"Hey @bestie, God didn't overlook you when He made you creative + kind + hilarious #YouAreLovedChallenge"

Prayer Journal: Talking to the God Who Knows Me

Hey, God already knows what's on your mind, but He really loves it when you just come to Him and share your truth. Take a moment to express how you're feeling and ask Him to remind you of how close He is and how much He cares.

Drop your prayer here:

"God, there are times when I just feel like..."

"But you say I'm not ignored. You see me, you get me, and you care. Just help me remember you're there, especially when I start to forget."

I have loved you with an everlasting love...

—Jeremiah 31:3 (NIV)

Week Two

EVERLASTING LOVE

et's be real—love can be *super* confusing.

We all crave it, but it's hard to define. People say they love you and then ghost you. Or maybe they only show love when you meet their expectations. So it makes sense that when we hear "God loves you," we might think... *"Okay, but what's the catch?"*

When we think about God's love, we often think about how other people have loved us. And let's face it—people don't always get it right.

But God's love? It's **different**. It's never fake. Never flaky. And never goes away.

Read Ephesians 2:4. (If you don't have a Bible with you, no problem! Just grab your phone and go to BibleGateway.com. You can search for any Bible verse there. Look for the NASB or NIV versions—they're easy to read and understand).

Even when we mess up, God offers us mercy. Not because we earned it—but because **He is love.**

Read Jeremiah 31:3

"I have loved you with an **everlasting love**; I have drawn you with **unfailing kindness.**" That means He had His eyes (and heart) set on you before you were born.

Read Psalm 145:8–9 & 1 John 4:19

- God's love is full of compassion.
- And we only *know* how to love because **He loved us first.**

So, here's the real question:

What's holding you back from fully receiving God's love?

- Are you scared it's too good to be true?
- Have you been hurt, and now it's hard to trust anyone—even God?
- Do you feel like you have to "clean yourself up" first?

Here's the truth: You don't have to **earn** God's love. You just have to **receive** it.

Reflect:

- What lies, wounds or fears might be blocking your heart?
- Where have you been keeping God at arm's length?

God isn't standing far off. He's chasing after you with grace, kindness, and an *everlasting* love.

Want more? Check these out:

- **Isaiah 54:10** – His love won't be shaken.
- **Psalm 86:5** – God is ready to forgive and overflowing with love.
- **Psalm 52:8** – His love is like a strong, rooted tree.

Prayer:

God, sometimes love feels confusing and complicated. People let me down, and it makes it hard to trust—even You. But I want to believe that Your love is real and that your love for me is strong. That it never walks away. Help me let go of the lies that say I'm not enough or that I have to earn Your love. Show me how to receive what You've already given so freely. Heal the parts of me that are scared, hurt, or unsure. Remind me that You've loved me from the beginning—with an everlasting, unfailing love. Draw me closer, God. I want to trust You more. Amen.

Discussion Questions:

How has the way people treated you shaped how you view God's love?

What's one lie or fear you've believed that makes it hard to fully trust God's love? And how does Scripture challenge that belief?

If you believed that God's love for you is unshakable and everlasting, how would that change how you see yourself and others?

Journaling Prompt – "No Strings Attached"

Write about this: **"What would it feel like to be fully loved without having to earn it?"**

Then, write a prayer asking God to help you experience His love in a real way this week.

Faith in Focus: Doodle Your Thoughts

Journaling Prompt – "Receiving Love Can Be Hard Sometimes"

Let's be real—being fully loved can feel kind of overwhelming. It might even be scary. Maybe you wonder if the love will last... or if you're really worth it.

Especially when it comes to God's love—it's big, constant, and never-ending. And that can be a lot to take in.

So let's talk about it:

- What feels hard or even a little scary about being totally loved—especially by God?
- What if you told Him about your fears or doubts? What might that feel like?

Take a moment to write out what's on your heart. God can handle it, and He's listening.

Faith in Focus: Doodle Your Thoughts

Social Challenge - #EverlastingLoveChallenge

Share a post or story that finishes this sentence:

"I'm letting go of _____ so I can receive God's love fully. #EverlastingLoveChallenge"

Or tag a friend and remind them:

"@yourfriend You are loved—completely and unconditionally. Just as you are. #EverlastingLoveChallenge"

Prayer Journal: A Prayer to Receive Love Without Earning It

God's love is never based on performance—it's a gift. You don't have to earn it or pretend to be perfect.

Use this space to pray honestly:

"God, sometimes I think I have to earn Your love. I struggle to believe You still love me when…"

"Help me let go and receive what You already gave freely. Open my heart to Your kindness and remind me that I am loved—just as I am."

For we are
God's handiwork...

—Ephesians 2:10 (NIV)

Week Three

MIRROR, MIRROR ON THE WALL

Let's talk about *you*—the way you see yourself.

We've already covered that God loves you like *crazy*. But... do *you* love you?

It might sound weird, but this is one of the hardest things for most of us. It's not that love isn't there—it's that we don't feel **worthy** of it. I've been there too. I remember the first time I had to film myself for a Bible study—I froze. I didn't want to see myself on video—and more than that, I didn't want anyone else to see me either. I had no idea how harsh I was being to myself... until that moment.

So let me ask:

What do you say to yourself when you look in the mirror?

"Not enough."
"Too much."
"Wish I looked different."

Does any of this sound familiar?

Read Luke 10:27. (If you don't have a Bible with you, no problem! Just grab your phone and go to BibleGateway.com. You can search for any Bible verse there. Look for the NASB or NIV versions— they're easy to read and understand).

Jesus says to love God, love your neighbor, and don't miss it: **love yourself.** That part often gets skipped. But if God calls you His masterpiece, who are you to argue with Him?

Read 1 John 4:19

- We love others *because* God loved us first.
- But how can we pass on that love if we're not even letting it into our own hearts?
- Perfectionism is a thief. It keeps whispering, *"You'll be enough when..."*

But guess what? God already calls you **beloved.** Period. No conditions.

Truth Check:

1. **1 Peter 3:3–4** – Your beauty is deeper than your selfies.
2. **Song of Songs 4:7** – "You are altogether beautiful." Yes, you.
3. **Psalm 139:13–14** – You were handmade, on purpose, with care.

Try This:

Next time you're in front of a mirror, and a negative thought pops into your mind, say out loud:

"Deliver me, Lord."

Then, replace that lie with truth from God's Word.

It's time to stop tearing yourself down. It's time to start loving who God made you to be. He sees **beauty**, **purpose**, and **strength** when He looks at you—and you should, too.

Prayer:

God, You are perfect and wonderful, and You said that I was made in Your image. Help me believe that, especially when I struggle to see it. Here's the truth, Lord—when I don't love myself, it becomes really hard to love others the way You want me to. Please give me the strength to change the way I think about myself. Help me see myself the way You see me so I can treat others with the love and kindness they deserve—because You love them just as much as You love me. Thank You for never giving up on me. Amen.

Discussion Questions:

What are some things you usually think or say about yourself when you look in the mirror? (Are those thoughts building you up—or tearing you down?)

Why do you think it's so hard to love ourselves the way God does? (What gets in the way for you personally?)

Which Bible verse from this week stood out to you the most—and how could it help you speak truth over yourself when you're struggling?

Journaling Prompt – "Through God's Eyes"

Look in the mirror and write down three honest thoughts you usually have about yourself.

Now, write what you think **God** says about you in those same moments. Ask Him to help you see yourself through His eyes.

Faith in Focus: Doodle Your Thoughts

Journaling Prompt – "Replacing the Lies"

We all have those thoughts that play on repeat in our minds—the ones that make us feel not good enough, unworthy, or just not okay. But here's the thing: those thoughts are *lies*, and it's time to shut them down with God's truth.

In the space below, write out **three lies** you've believed about yourself.

Then, right next to each one, write a **truth from the Bible** that shows who you *really* are in God's eyes.

Example:
Lie: I'm not good enough.
Truth: *"You are God's masterpiece." – Ephesians 2:10 (NLT)*

Ready? Be honest and bold—truth brings freedom.

The Lie	God's Truth

Social Challenge - #MirrorTruthChallenge

Take a mirror selfie (yep, this is your brave moment!) and share one truth from Scripture that you're choosing to believe about yourself.

"I am fearfully and wonderfully made. #MirrorTruthChallenge #YouAreLovedStudy"

Or tag a friend and remind them:

"@friend You are more than enough—just the way God made you #MirrorTruthChallenge"

Prayer Journal: A Prayer to See Myself Through God's Eyes

God sees you with love, purpose, and beauty. Even when you don't feel it. Use this prayer space to be real with Him and invite His truth to take root in your heart.

"God, I often tell myself..."

"But You say I am…"

"Help me believe it. Teach me to speak truth over myself instead of lies. Thank You for loving me completely—even when I struggle to love myself."

Love
one
another.

—John 13: 34 (NIV)

Week Four

LIVE OUT LOVE

We've spent the past few weeks talking about how much God loves *you*, who you are in Him, and how to love yourself like He does.

Now, it's time to live it out.

When I was getting ready to speak at a women's conference, I prayed and felt God asking me one thing over and over again:

"Do they know they are loved?"

That simple question changed everything. Around the same time, I was learning two big truths in a theology class:

1. We're called to **live holy lives.**
2. **Judging others? That's God's job—not ours.**

So, how do we take *everything* we've learned and start walking it out?

Read 1 Corinthians 13:1–13. (If you don't have a Bible with you, no problem! Just grab your phone and go to BibleGateway.com. You can search for any Bible verse there. Look for the NASB or NIV versions—they're easy to read and understand).

Paul says you can have *all* the world's smarts, faith, and talent, but if you don't have love, you're just making noise.

Love isn't jealous, rude, selfish, or mean. It's **kind, patient, forgiving,** and **real.**

Loving others isn't always easy—especially when:

- You're exhausted
- Someone pushes your buttons
- People are just *being people*

I once asked a pastor for advice after I totally lost my patience. He told me to watch out for **triggers** and give myself timeouts when needed. That stuck with me. Because sometimes, love looks like taking a breath, walking away, or asking God for help *before* you react.

Imagine this:

What if we all showed up at school, practice, or home with God's love in our hearts? That kind of love can shift the atmosphere. It can soften hearts, heal wounds, and bring hope.

And the best part? You don't have to be perfect to make an impact. Start small. Start where you are. Just **start with love.**

Prayer:

God, Thank You for meeting me in this study. Thank You for showing me that I am deeply, unconditionally, and forever loved by You. Help me hold onto that truth when I feel insecure, unworthy, or forgotten. Change how I see myself to love others with the same grace You've shown me. Give me the courage to live out Your love—in my words, choices, and actions. Even when it's hard, remind me to pause, pray, and trust You. Fill my heart so full of Your love that it overflows into every part of my life. I want to walk in love, live purposefully, and reflect on who You are. Thank You for calling me Yours. In Jesus' name, Amen.

Discussion Questions:

What does "living out love" look like in your everyday life—at school, at home, or with friends? (Where is it easiest, and where is it hardest?)

When you're tired, frustrated, or triggered, what helps you pause instead of react? (Have you ever tried giving yourself a spiritual "timeout"?)

What's one small way you can show God's love to someone this week—even if it's hard or uncomfortable? (Think simple: a kind word, listening, forgiving, or just showing up.)

Journaling Prompt - "Love in Action"

Write down three specific places or situations where it's hard for you to love others (home, school, a certain friend group, etc.).

Now ask God:

"What does it look like to love like *You* in that situation?"

Challenge yourself to show one intentional act of love this week in one of those hard places.

Live Out Love

Faith in Focus: Doodle Your Thoughts

Journaling Prompt – "One Small Act"

Let's be honest—some people are just *hard* to love. Maybe they've hurt your feelings, get on your nerves, or just make life more complicated. But God still calls us to love them—even when it's not easy.

Take a minute to think about this:

- Who's one person in your life right now that's tough to love?
- What's one small thing you could do to show them God's love this week—on purpose?

Write it down below, then challenge yourself to actually do it. God can use even the smallest act of kindness in a big way.

Faith in Focus: Doodle Your Thoughts

Social Challenge - #LiveOutLoveChallenge

Post a pic or Story of something that represents loving others well—it could be as simple as helping a friend, writing a kind note, or choosing not to react in anger.

Caption it with:

"Letting God's love move through me #LiveOutLoveChallenge #YouAreLovedStudy"

Or tag a friend and encourage them to do one loving thing today with you!

Prayer Journal: A Prayer to Love Others the Way God Loves Me

Loving others like God does doesn't mean being perfect—it means being willing. Use this space to ask for His help.

"God, it's hard for me to love when…"

"Fill me with Your love so I can live it out in…"

_____

_____

_____

_____

_____

_____

_____

"Help me love with patience, kindness, and grace—even when it's difficult. Use me as a reflection of Your heart."

_____

_____

_____

_____

_____

_____

_____

Conclusion

Throughout this journey, we've uncovered the powerful truth that **God deeply loves you**—not because of what you do, but simply because of who He is. His love is consistent, unconditional, and personal. It doesn't fade when life gets hard or when others disappoint you. Even in moments of doubt or struggle, God's love remains steady and sure.

We also looked inward and faced the honest truth about how we see ourselves. In a world full of pressure and comparison, it's easy to believe lies about our worth. But God calls you His masterpiece— created with purpose, beauty, and intention. Loving yourself isn't prideful; it's living in agreement with God's truth.

And now, you're invited to take what you've learned and live it out. Loving others with patience, grace, and kindness isn't always easy—but it's exactly what the world needs. You don't have to be perfect to make an impact. You just need to show up, stay rooted in God's love, and be willing to reflect it in everything you do.

So here's the big takeaway:

You are loved. You are chosen. You are enough.

Let that truth sink deep. Let it shape how you see yourself and how you treat others. No matter where life takes you, remember that love is your starting point and will lead you to your purpose.

What does "You Are Loved" mean to you personally?

Write a letter to your future self, reminding yourself how God sees you.

List 5 truths from the study that you want to remember.

Faith in Focus: Doodle Your Thoughts

Faith in Focus: Doodle Your Thoughts

Faith in Focus: Doodle Your Thoughts

Faith in Focus: Doodle Your Thoughts

YOU ARE LOVED
Small Group Leader's Guide

Overview

This four-week Bible study is all about helping teens:

- Understand God's love for them.
- Discover their identity in Him.
- Learn to love themselves as God does.
- Take that love into the world and live it out.

Each week includes a short teaching, Scripture readings, journaling, discussion questions, and a challenge.

Leader Tips

1. Set the vibe

Create a space that feels safe, chill, and welcoming. Bring snacks, play music when they arrive, or let them decorate journals—whatever fits your group. The goal? Help them *relax and show up as they are.*

2. Be real

Share your own stories—especially moments when you've wrestled with the same things. Teens connect best with authenticity, not perfection.

3. Let them talk

Some teens might be quiet at first. Give space for silence. Ask open-ended questions. If they don't respond right away, that's okay—God's still working.

4. Keep it rooted in Scripture

Teens are bombarded with messages about who they are and what love means. Always bring them back to God's Word as the ultimate truth.

Make sure to:

Encourage journaling with fun pens or printed prompts.

Pray *with* and *for* your group regularly.

Be available outside of group time if someone needs to talk.

Use the social challenges to keep momentum during the week.

WEEKLY BREAKDOWN

Week One – OVERLOOKED

Big Idea:
God sees you, knows you, and has never overlooked you.

Opening Question:
Have you ever felt invisible or left out? What did that feel like?

Read Together:
Isaiah 43:4, Psalm 139:1–18, Isaiah 49:16, John 3:16.

Discussion Starters:
Why do you think it's so easy to feel overlooked—even by God?

Which verse hit you the most and why?

What's something that helps you *remember* you matter to God?

Challenge:
Post (or write) a truth about your identity in God this week. #YouAreLovedChallenge

Week Two – EVERLASTING LOVE

Big Idea:
God's love is forever. You can't lose it or earn it.

Opening Question:
What's one word you'd use to describe love? Why?

Read Together:
Ephesians 2:4, Jeremiah 31:3, Psalm 145:8–9, 1 John 4:19.

Discussion Starters:
Have you ever felt like love had to be earned?

What holds you back from fully receiving God's love?

What do you think it means that God's love is "everlasting"?

Challenge:
Let go of one lie and replace it with truth.
#EverlastingLoveChallenge

Week Three - MIRROR, MIRROR ON THE WALL

Big Idea:
You were made in God's image—and that makes you beautiful and valuable.

Opening Question:
What's something you love about someone else that you wish you had?

Read Together:
Luke 10:27, 1 John 4:19, 1 Peter 3:3–4, Song of Songs 4:7, Psalm 139:13–14.

Discussion Starters:
What's the hardest thing for you to believe about yourself?

Why do you think it's easier to be kind to others than to ourselves?

How do you think God sees you?

Challenge:
Speak one truth over yourself every day this week.
#MirrorTruthChallenge

Week Four - LIVE OUT LOVE

Big Idea:
Let's take God's love into our world—one small act at a time.

Opening Question:
Who's someone that's really hard for you to love right now?

Read Together:
1 Corinthians 13:1–13.

Discussion Starters:
What makes it hard to love others?

How can you pause and respond with grace instead of reacting with anger?

What would it look like to "live out love" in your life this week?

Challenge:
Do one intentional act of love this week.
#LiveOutLoveChallenge

About the Author

Lisa Fahey is an author and speaker with over twenty years of experience working with youth, adults, and women in the Church. She is the author of *Rise Up, Women of God, A Scripture Study on 1 John and 2 John*; *Simply, A Women's Study on Ecclesiastes*; *Simply Advent*; *Just As You Are, How Your Testimony Can Impact People In Ways You Never Thought Possible*; *Restored: From Ordinary to Extraordinary*; and *Simply Lent: A Journey of Reflection and Renewal with Jesus*.

All are meant to inspire, encourage, and empower readers in their journey with God. Lisa draws on real-life stories and moments with God to inspire and encourage others.

At the age of 21, Lisa lost her first husband, which forever changed her approach to God and His Word. Through her work, she shares how God helped her to grow and rise up as a woman of God, even during the trials of life.

Although "life is hard and messy," Lisa is able to show her readers through her Bible studies and books that the key to experiencing life completely is to follow their calling by serving God.

If this book has blessed you, please share the message with others by posting on social media using #youareloved

Website
www.lisafahey.com

Publishing
farmhousepublishings@gmail.com

Follow Your Call Coaching
www.lisafahey.com/follow-your-call-coaching

Podcast
Lisa Fahey Ministry (Apple & Spotify)

Facebook
Christian Professional Women On Purpose - Lisa Fahey

Instagram
lisafaheyministry

OTHER TITLES BY LISA FAHEY

SIMPLY: A WOMEN'S BIBLE STUDY ON ECCLESIASTES

A six week study of Ecclesiastes. This book of wisdom teaches us that living simply is the secret to experiencing life to the fullest.

RISE UP, WOMEN OF GOD: A STUDY OF 1 JOHN & 2 JOHN

This six week study of 1 and 2 John are the ideal Epistles to guide us through life's questions and confusing times.

SIMPLY ADVENT: A DAILY DEVOTIONAL TO PREPARE THE WAY FOR JESUS

Advent helps us simplify the chaos by preparing our hearts for Christmas.

JUST AS YOU ARE: HOW YOUR TESTIMONY CAN IMPACT PEOPLE IN WAYS YOU NEVER THOUGHT POSSIBLE

Your testimony can reach people for Christ in ways you never thought possible.

RESTORED: FROM ORDINARY TO EXTRAORDINARY

Becoming the person God intended you to be... Extraordinary

SIMPLY LENT: A JOURNEY OF REFLECTION AND RENEWAL WITH JESUS

The season of Lent encourages us to pause, reflect, and reconnect with God's purpose for our lives, guiding us through everyday life.